What You Don't Know About End of Life Planning

What You Don't Know About End of Life Planning:

A guide to discover the death-positive movement, exploring your options, and living and dying with intention

Felicia M. Barlow Clar

©2021 by Felicia M. Barlow Clar, All rights reserved. Copyright and other intellectual property laws protect these materials.

Copyright is the basis for our inspired creativity. It protects and promotes free speech. Thank you for complying with copyright and intellectual property laws by not reprinting, reproducing, or distributing this workbook in any manner without the prior written consent of the copyright holder, except in the case of brief excerpts in critical reviews or articles.

Visit our website at www.celebratingthedash.com
dba Epilogue Tributes
Barclar Entertainment, LLC
Annapolis, MD 21401
USA

Cover design by Erin Foggoa

ISBN (paperback): 978-1-7368251-0-5
ISBN (PDF): 978-1-7368251-1-2

While the author has made every effort to provide accurate internet addresses at the time of publication, the author does not assume any responsibility for errors or changes that may occur after publication. Further the author and publisher does not have any control over nor assumes any responsibility for third-party websites or their content.

This workbook is NOT a legal document and does NOT replace the expertise of an attorney, financial advisor, medical practitioner, or others. The author has created a blank workbook for you to use at your own risk, and she has no control over the information you enter. The author and publisher shall in no event be held liable to any party for any direct, indirect, punitive, special, incidental, or other consequential damages arising directly or indirectly from any use of this material, which is provided "as is" and without warranties. The author and publisher assume no liability, responsibility, or damage of any kind as the result of the use or misuse of personal or protected information, such as financial information or other sensitive and/or confidential information you may enter. Please exercise extreme care and protection of this document once you have filled it in.

The presence of fear is always an invitation to love more.

~ Anita Moorjani

End-of-Life Planning

Congratulations on taking this very important step. You've made the best decision for yourself and your loved ones. When we consider it, we plan for just about every major life event, from weddings and vacations to baby showers and retirement. Yet we ignore one of the most important transitions of them all.

End-of-life planning can be a sensitive and uncomfortable topic. Pondering our own mortality is something few of us want to face. But death doesn't discriminate. Getting our affairs in order is advisable for *everyone*. When we don't, we run the risk of leaving behind a mess, which can cause arguments and family conflict. It often overwhelms and adds to tremendous grief. Something few of us intend to do.

It is with this awareness and experience that my workbooks have been thoughtfully prepared. I am among a growing movement of people who have been led to empower generations and advocate for reclaiming our end of life and the way in which we want to be remembered and memorialized. I support the many alternatives and choices being presented and encourage you to seek out these varying resources beyond funeral homes and grief counseling until you find what resonates with YOU.

I believe this pre-planning document will help you to organize, while supporting your loved ones and reducing unnecessary suffering in the face of grief. Please use this planning book to write down key information to outline your wishes upon your passing. When completed, you have an opportunity to communicate your desires and love while you are still alive. Make the conversation about planning ahead, instead of dying.

This book should be stored in a secure but familiar place, preferably one that is fireproof. Safety deposit boxes and safes are not advisable locations. This plan needs to be accessible. I suggest using a pencil for those areas that may need to be periodically updated. You should revisit this book annually or whenever a major life event happens (ex., marriage, divorce). *Remember to update your beneficiaries, as well.* There are too many stories of legal battles, often among family, over what somebody meant to do but didn't.

You may also want to provide a copy of this book to your attorney. At the very least, please inform your attorney and/or Executor where this book is kept.

This workbook is not a legal document, so checklists should only be viewed as recommendations. Please seek out the appropriate experts for sound advice.

An Executor should be someone you trust will follow your wishes and instructions.

Have you appointed an Executor? ____yes ____no

Name of Executor (aka, personal representative) and contact information:

My Estate attorney:

Legal firm:

Location:

Phone number:

Other trusted decision makers:

Professionals to Notify

Financial advisor/CPA:

Insurance agent(s):

Doctor(s):

Dentist:

Employer:

Clergy:

Life Celebrant (ex. *Epilogue Tributes*):

Legal Decisions

Experts recommend a few legal documents to help make life easier for your beneficiaries. Most are a complement to this workbook and take care of the legal decisions that need to be made and documented.

The LGBTQ+ community, in particular, needs to make sure their legal documents and desires are in place. There are countless heartbreaking stories of family conflicts, loved ones and partners being left out, and personal choices being ignored due to an omission of legal documents. In more than half the states, there is a statutory obligation for survivors to honor the written wishes of the deceased. One of the most useful laws is for you to name a "Designated Agent" for body disposition and end-of-life plans. You can find details for your state and sample forms through the Funeral Consumers Alliance: https://funerals.org/?consumers=legal-right-make-decisions-funeral

A *Revocable Living Trust* is the centerpiece of a complete estate plan and has gained widespread popularity in the United States. It helps avoid probate, save money, protect heirs, and preserve privacy, as it prevents the details of your estate from becoming available to the public. A Revocable Living Trust can be changed at any time, differing from an *Irrevocable Trust*, which can not be modified without the consent of the beneficiaries. It is erroneous to believe you must have great wealth to put a Revocable Living Trust in place (that is typically an irrevocable trust). **Please consult an attorney to see if this is something that will be a benefit for your estate.**

I have:

☐ Designated Agent (specify:): _____

☐ Revocable Living Trust

☐ Revocable Living Trust has an "Incapacity Clause"

☐ Last Will and Testament

☐ Irrevocable Trust

☐ Detailed what I would like done with my possessions

☐ Possession distribution detailed on my Personal Property Memorandum

☐ Pour-Over Will

☐ Durable Power of Attorney

☐ Financial Power of Attorney

☐ Advanced Medical Directive

☐ Do Not Resuscitate Orders (DNR)

☐ Made plans for dependent care

☐ Prepared legal documents/guardianship required for minor dependents

☐ Informed family members of minor dependent guardianship

☐ Social Security benefits available for disabled child over the age of 18

☐ Plans and consideration made for any Special Needs dependents (note here):

☐ Made guardianship arrangements for my pet(s)

☐ Created a Pet Trust, if available in my state

For more information: https://www.aspca.org/pet-care/pet-planning/pet-trust-primer

☐ Made other financial arrangements for the care of my pet(s) (specify):

☐ Informed family members of pet(s) guardianship
☐ Made provisions for caretakers to get access to funds
☐ Storage location for this workbook is fireproof? ____yes ____no
☐ Copy and/or directives for this workbook's location given to:

You can obtain quick and easy legal documents online that are good in all 50 states, typically at very reasonable fees. Sites include Suze Orman's Will & Trust Kit, Mama Bear, Legal Zoom, or Legal Shield.

There are also qualified local attorneys who specialize in estate planning. Many provide free Estate Planning Seminars.

Health Care Decisions

Death is a natural and sacred part of life. Too often we ignore the desires of our loved ones until it is too late. Reports show that 90% of those terminally ill have expressed the desire to pass away at home. Yet most die in hospitals. Planning ahead can ensure a more comfortable passing.

Advance care planning involves medical decisions that are often difficult. Making decisions *before* you face a health crisis is pertinent. Having conversations with your

Executor and loved ones is the best way to convey your decisions, especially if you become incapacitated.

For some communities, such as the Black community, making decisions about who can speak for you, desires for treatment, and how you want to be treated at the end can be empowering while you're still in good health. Given the historical exploitation of Blacks in medical research, often carried out without consent, making your own decisions is an act of freedom and justice.

I have:

☐ An Advanced Medical Directive and a trusted person to convey my health decisions should I become incapacitated.

☐ My Health Care Decision Maker is:

☐ Detailed my life support desires in my Advanced Medical Directive (aka, Living Will)

☐ Been made aware that hospice is covered by private insurance and by Medicare and Medicaid in the United States.

It is important to know that anybody can refer you to hospice. You are not required to go through a doctor's office, and some may prefer to avoid a doctor for various reasons.

☐ I am aware anybody can refer me to hospice — doctor, nurse, social worker, clergy, family, friends, or myself.

☐ Home hospice is my preference: ____yes ____no

There are differing Advanced Directives you should be aware of. I highly recommend *Five Wishes* as a complement to this workbook. It is a thorough directive that covers personal, emotional, and spiritual matters in regard to health care and medical treatment.

For more information:
https://fivewishes.org/shop/order/product/five-wishes-advance-directive

☐ I have completed the *Five Wishes* Advanced Care Directive.*
    *Separate fee

Compassion & Choices is another invaluable resource for understanding the expanding options for end-of-life care. They are the United State's oldest nonprofit organization working to ensure individuals, not the healthcare system, is in charge. While the medical field has made incredible advances, they also present a dilemma for those with a terminal illness. This includes: How much treatment is enough? And how do you want to live out your final years? Months? Days?

Compassion & Choices' website includes many topics: assisted living, pain care, palliative and hospice care, and medical aid in dying. For more information:
https://compassionandchoices.org

☐ I have reviewed the free resources available at:
https://compassionandchoices.org/end-of-life-planning

☐ I have read Compassion and Choices' *Finish Strong**, a guide to achieving the positive end-of-life experience you want and deserve.

*Separate fee

☐ I have discussed the many end-of-life options with my attorney and loved ones.
☐ I have made my end-of-life desires known and documented them with my attorney.

These conversations may be very difficult to approach. A conversation is love in action. There are resources to help here too. If you need guidance, visit:
https://theconversationproject.org

Care and Treatment/Disposition of Your Body

There are options open to you for the care and treatment of your body after death. Unfortunately, many are still unknown to the masses. A funeral home/service is simply one choice. In most states, the requirement to have a funeral home involved is limited. All options can be dignified and affordable.

The first consideration is deciding how you want your body to be cared for before final disposition. Emerging alternatives include the resurgence of home-based rituals. This is care once handled by family members pre Civil War, including body washing, which can be one of the most sacred acts of love.

There are non-medical service providers who can assist, often called End-of-Life Doulas or Death Doulas. This field will change how we handle end-of-life care and needs, as the medical establishment changes and we age. Doulas niche their offerings, so make sure you seek out a few and find one that fits your needs. They not only can help in hospice, but they often assist families and Executors with after death needs, such as paperwork and home organizing.

☐ I prefer my loved ones care for my body at home (ex. body washing ritual).
☐ Special instructions for the care and treatment of my body are:

☐ Personal rituals and/or spiritual practices I'd like incorporated are (include music, colors, flowers, scents, crystals, etc.):

☐ My preferred End-of-Life Doula and contact information is:

After the care of my body, I would like arrangements made for disposition as follows:

☐ I prefer (check one): ____burial ____entombment ____green burial ____cremation ____Aquamation ____open-air funeral pyre ____other (specify):

☐ My clothing preference is: ____something I own ____something new
Specify:

☐ Immediate burial
☐ Direct cremation
☐ Witness cremation (specify who):

☐ Viewing (check one): ____private ____public
☐ Casket: ____open ____ closed
☐ I prefer _____ number of viewings.
☐ I am aware embalming is not required in most circumstances.
☐ I prefer NOT to be embalmed, if possible.
☐ Green burial. Preference at (circle one): designated cemetery, wood preserve, private property, or other. Specify location:

☐ Shroud/wrap preference for a green burial. This can be a blanket or some other material you hold dear (specify):

☐ Preference of casket, if buried (check one): ____wood ____steel ____fiberglass ____biodegradable ____wicker ____nothing fancy ____other (specify):

☐ My loved ones can craft a personalized casket.
☐ I have prepaid for my cemetery plot, mausoleum, or columbarium (circle one).
Located at:

☐ Cemetery preference, if not prepaid (availability will need to be researched):

☐ I prefer to be placed in a mausoleum/entombment within the cemetery.

☐ Preference of urn*, if cremated (check one): ____wood ____metal ____stone ____artisan piece ____jewelry piece ____biodegradable ____other (specify):

☐ My loved ones can craft a personalized urn.
☐ I would like _____ to be given my remains.

☐ I prefer my cremains be disposed/scattered in a specific manner/location:
____sea ____coral reef ____tree roots ____garden ____wood preserve ____mushrooms ____spaceflight ____fireworks ____compost ____jewelry ____artwork ____private property ____a variety of favorite locations ____other (specify):

Specify the variety of locations, if this is your choice. Provide as many details as possible, including country and/or significance, so that your cremains are disposed of as you desire. *Legal restrictions may apply.*

If you desire your ashes be scattered outside the United States, please talk to your Executor and/or Designated Agent. Calls should be made to the appropriate Embassy to see if there are any restrictions. Most countries welcome this. ***A TSA approved urn and cremation certificate will be needed.***

If your remains are to be disposed on private property, complete this section:

☐ I have researched the city/state/county laws for private property disposition.
☐ Private property address for my remains is:

☐ I have the Owner's permission legally documented.
☐ Name of the Owner granting permission:

☐ Owner/Grantee's contact information:

Donation to Science/Donation of Organs

Many medical schools depend on generous individuals to donate their bodies upon passing, benefitting science, education, and future generations. Special arrangements, consent, and care must be taken, often within a specific timeframe, to participate. Therefore, it is very important for your relatives or survivors to be informed *beforehand* of your plans, so arrangements are carried out accordingly.

It is possible to conduct a viewing and funeral, but no embalming should occur, and events should be held immediately. Often, these medical schools will pay for transport of the body and/or return cremated remains to next of kin, or a designated representative, within 12 to 36 months of donation.

There is a great need for organ donation, as well. Men, women, and children await lifesaving organ transplants every year. Each registration can save a number of lives. However, it is not possible to donate specific organs *and* your body.

Put "n/a" if this is not applicable to you: _____

☐ I am donating my body to science.
☐ I understand all major religions support donation as a final act of compassion and generosity.
☐ I have discussed my plans for body donation with my relatives, Executor, and /or Designated Agent.
☐ The program I am donating *my body* to:

☐ Contact information for my program:

☐ I have completed a Donor Authorization form for this program.
☐ I have a Uniform Donor Card in my wallet.

☐ I have chosen to donate *my organs*.
☐ I have registered with www.BeaDonor.org

☐ I will be donating specific body parts to (ex.: eyes to Lions' Eye Bank):

☐ My decision to be an organ donor is noted on my state driver's license.
☐ I carry an Organ Donor Card in my wallet.
☐ I have discussed my plans for organ donation with my relatives, Executor, and/or Designated Agent.
☐ If remains are returned as a part of my chosen program, I would like them to be given to _____ when the program is complete.

Celebration of Life/Memorial Service

For centuries, funerals were handled at home by family. The logistics of the Civil War necessitated the advent of funeral homes and embalming. In a step towards healing and acceptance of death, *home funerals* are now seeing a resurgence. They require planning, preparation, and knowledge of your state laws, and often cost very little. There are resources available to assist families with personalized arrangements. The *National Home Funeral Alliance* offers insights on how to care for the body at home.

A *Celebration of Life* is a service where a body is not present and can be done at any time, almost anywhere, and can vary in expenditure. I created my company because I saw the enormous need for personalization when working with a funeral home. My family was handed templates and services that simply did not fit my loved ones' life story. Having to make decisions, plan details, and write eulogies, among other tasks, in a limited amount of time while experiencing loss, was both overwhelming and stressful. I now assist in creating a personal, memorable, and joyous service that honors life and legacy, giving loved ones the space to grieve. There are many service providers modernizing the funeral industry.

As a pandemic has made us aware, an immediate gathering is not always possible (or necessary). In this scenario, you have options, including an immediate burial or direct cremation. A Celebration of Life service can follow at a later date. *Virtual vigils* and/or gatherings, as well as video tributes, are also an option, albeit limited and not the same as in-person services with human touch. I highly recommend hiring event/video professionals for these options, as unfortunately, these are not an expertise I've seen handled well by funeral directors.

When all is said and done, there are services available to fit nearly any situation and budget. I highly recommend visiting the Funeral Consumers Alliance website and researching the risks of prepaying funerals and laws regarding transparency in pricing. Burial and cremation expenses can vary *drastically* for the same service in the same state.

My ideal service:

☐ I prefer a home funeral.
☐ My "care community" to assist with my home funeral is/are:

☐ I prefer a traditional funeral.
☐ I prefer a personalized and joyful Celebration of Life Service.
☐ I expect expenses for my Celebration of Life service or funeral to be paid from:

☐ Full details for my memorial service are detailed in my companion workbook: *A Celebration of Life Planner: Making Your Memories Your Legacy.*

☐ Officiant requested:

☐ Officiant's contact information:

Biographical Information

Much of the following information will be needed for the Death Certificate. It can also be helpful in writing an obituary and planning your personalized Celebration of Life.

Full name (official first, middle, and last on birth certificate):

Maiden name, if applicable:

Any aliases, nicknames, or "also known as":

Social Security Number:
Date of birth (month/day/year):
Birthplace (city/state/country):

Current residence (street, city, county, state, zip code):

Current phone number:
Current cell phone number:
Sex (*biological*): ____male ____female ____other (specify, if prefer):
Gender (*cultural preference*):

Specific pronouns you would like to be addressed by (check one):
____he/him ____she/her ____they/them ____zie/zim ____ve/ver ____other (specify): _____

Race:

Marital Status (check one): ____ single ____married ____divorced ____remarried ____widow/widower ____life partner/domestic partner

Father's full name, date of birth, and birthplace:

Mother's full maiden name, date of birth, and birthplace:

Education (highest):

Occupation:

Business/Industry:

Employer:

Employer Address:

Marital History

Surviving spouse's name (include maiden name, if applicable):

Marriage date:

Location of wedding:

Does this location hold any other significance for you?

☐ Social Security benefits available for surviving spouse

Previous Spouse(s)

Include full name, date of marriage and state/country, divorce finalization date and state/country, current address and phone number (if known), and any significant notes.

☐ Previous spouse:

☐ Previous spouse:

Veteran Information

Thank you for your service & sacrifice!

☐ Served in the U.S. Armed Forces, or other country (specify):

☐ Active Duty in the U.S. Armed Forces, or other country (specify):

Branch of Service:

Rank and Service Number:

Date and place of enlistment:

Dates served:

Date of discharge:

☐ If Active Duty, local contact where burial benefits can be arranged:

Veterans Administration Claim Number:

War/Conflicts/Tours of Duty:

Commendations and medals received:

☐ I would like a military funeral.
☐ I want to be buried at a Veterans cemetery.
Preferred Veterans cemetery location:

Information/inscription for my Veteran's grave marker:

Religious Information

If atheist or agnostic, you can skip this section or provide details on how you would like to be memorialized. A complete, personalized service can be thought out in **my companion workbook: *A Celebration of Life Planner: Making Your Memories Your Legacy.***

Services requested: _____religious _____ non-religious
Religion:

Type of service: ____public ____private

Preferred house of worship:

Address and telephone:

Clergy, officiant, or layperson:

Contact information:

Instructions for Dependents and/or Pets

To ensure your beloved dependents and/or pet(s) are well cared for, complete this section, if applicable.

Name of dependent(s):

Are any of your dependents adults with special needs? Explain. Include doctors, medications, group home care, etc.

Who will have legal guardianship of your non-adult dependent(s)?

Who will take care of your adult dependent(s)?

Detail any special dietary restrictions for dependent(s):

Who will take care of the immediate needs of your pet(s)?

Who will become the full-time guardian of your pet(s)?

Note: Animals grieve too. A piece of your clothing, with your scent, may bring comfort to your pet(s) upon your passing.

Pet's Name:
____dog ____cat ____other (specify):
Diet:

Medical issues:

Typical sleep/favorite bedding:
Favorite toy:
Cage to transport: ____yes ____no
Where can these items be found?

Pet's Name:
____dog ____cat ____other (specify):
Diet:

Medical issues:

Typical sleep/favorite bedding:

Favorite toy:

Cage to transport: ____yes ____no

Where can these items be found?

Pet's Name:

____dog ____cat ____other (specify):

Diet:

Medical issues:

Typical sleep/favorite bedding:

Favorite toy:

Cage to transport: ____yes ____no

Where can these items be found?

Veterinarian's name, address, and telephone:

Location of Documents

Your Executor, Medical Director, and family members will need to know where your documents are kept if there is a medical emergency or death. Note where each is located below. Include an account number or other reference and any notes. Put "n/a" if not applicable to you. Additional lines are included if you have items to add.

DOCUMENT	LOCATION	NOTES
BIRTH CERTIFICATE		
CHILDREN'S BIRTH CERTIFICATE(S)		
ADOPTION RECORDS		
MARRIAGE CERTIFICATE		
DIVORCE DECREE		
PRENUPTIAL AGREEMENT		
LAST WILL & TESTAMENT		
BODY DONOR AGREEMENT		
ORGAN DONOR DIRECTIVE(S)		
CEMETERY/MAUSOLEUM PLOT DEED		
TRUST DOCUMENTS		
PERSONAL PROPERTY MEMORANDUM		
POUR-OVER WILL		
DURABLE POWER OF ATTORNEY		
FINANCIAL POWER OF ATTORNEY		
ADVANCED MEDICAL DIRECTIVE		
DO NOT RESUSCITATE ORDER (DNR)		

DOCUMENT	LOCATION	NOTES
FIVE WISHES DOCUMENTATION		
A CELEBRATION OF LIFE PLANNER: Making Your Memories Your Legacy		
MEDICAL RECORDS		
CHILDREN'S MEDICAL RECORDS		
MEDICAL RECORDS FOR PET(S)		
HOME DEED(S)		
MORTGAGE PAPERS/LOAN		
VEHICLE TITLE(S)		
VACATION CLUB/TIMESHARE		
VETERAN FORM(S)		
MILITARY DISCHARGE PAPERS		
MILITARY ID		
SOCIAL SECURITY CARD		
DRIVER'S LICENSE		
PASSPORT (COUNTRY)		
CITIZENSHIP/NATURALIZATION DOCUMENTS		
INCOME TAX RECORDS		
LIFE INSURANCE POLICIES		
HEALTH INSURANCE POLICIES		
LONG TERM CARE &/OR DISABILITY INSURANCE		
AUTO INSURANCE		
HOME/RENTERS/PROPERTY INSURANCE		
DISASTER INSURANCE		

DOCUMENT	LOCATION	NOTES
UMBRELLA/LIABILITY INSURANCE		
BUSINESS DOCUMENTS		
PET(S) INSURANCE		
RESUME/CV/BIO		
SAFE & COMBINATION		

Banking and Assets

Record financial institution(s) and account number(s) or other references below, and any notes. Recent account statements should be easily accessible for your Executor. Put "n/a" if not applicable.

☐ Location of financial records:

☐ Savings account(s):

☐ Checking account(s) / Checkbook(s):

☐ Safe deposit box: ____yes ____no
☐ Safe deposit box number: _____
Institution name and address for safe deposit box:

Location of safe deposit box key:

☐ Post Office Box: ____yes ____no
☐ P.O. Box number: _____
P.O. Box location/address:

Location of P.O. Box key:

☐ Mortgage/Rent:

☐ Alimony/Child Support:

☐ Loans:

☐ Money Market Account(s):

☐ Certificate(s) of Deposit:

☐ Mutual Funds:

☐ Stocks and Bonds:

☐ Annuities:

☐ Government Bonds:

☐ Retirement Plans (ex. 401K, IRA):

☐ Profit-Sharing:

☐ Pension:

☐ Automobile/Boat/Recreational Vehicle Loans:

Location of account statements:

Location of tax records:

☐ **Credit Cards:**

ISSUED BY	LAST 4 DIGITS	TOLL-FREE NUMBER

☐ **Miscellaneous Valuables (ex. artwork, jewelry, equipment):**

DESCRIPTION	LOCATION	NET VALUE

The following is a list of real estate I own:

RESIDENTIAL/COMMERCIAL	LOCATION	MORTGAGE

The following loans or gifts have been made to beneficiaries that are intended to be treated as advance distributions of their share of my estate:

BENEFICIARY	LOAN AMOUNT/GIFT	VALUE

Home Security

☐ My Executor has a key(s) to my house.
☐ I have an alarm or security system.
☐ My Executor has a security access code to enter my house.
Security account number: _____

Name of my security company:

Contact for my security company:

☐ I own a car(s), truck, and/or motorcycle.
☐ Make/model of my vehicle is:

☐ Make/model of my vehicle is:

☐ Make/model of my vehicle is:

☐ My Executor has a key to my vehicle(s).

If Executor does not have keys to your house or vehicle(s), where will they find these?

Digital Accounts and Online Passwords

Identify all devices and accounts and how someone you trust can access these. This is especially important for social media accounts. Some social media accounts will allow you to set "memorialization settings" (i.e., Facebook) and decide what happens to your account upon your passing; make sure you set these up now.

DEVICE/ACCOUNT	USERNAME	PASSWORD
COMPUTER		
INTERNET PROVIDER		
EMAIL PROVIDER		
CELL PHONE		
FACEBOOK		
TWITTER		
INSTAGRAM		
LINKED IN		
PINTEREST		
ONLINE BANKING		
MEDICAL (Primary)		
AMAZON		
CREDIT CARD:		
CREDIT CARD:		
CREDIT CARD:		
CREDIT CARD:		
WEBSITE		
BLOG		
ONLINE PASSWORD STORAGE		

DEVICE/ACCOUNT	USERNAME	PASSWORD
HOME SECURITY		

☐ I store my online passwords on a storage website (ex. Last Pass).

Name of online storage website is:

_____ has access to my passwords on this site.

Business Property

If you own a business, specifically if self-employed or a solopreneur, including some basic information will help your Executor handle details to sell or close your business. If you have a business partner and/or are incorporated, please note information that may ease the transition. If you are a creative and own patents, copyrights, trademarks, or expect royalties, please note here.

BUSINESS NAME &/or DESCRIPTION	BUSINESS ENTITY (ex: LLC)	VALUE

☐ I have a business partner.

Name of my business partner:

Business partner's contact information:

Life Review

In addition to helping create an informative obituary, these details can be used to notify organizations and people who will want to know about your death. Drafting your own obituary is advised and explained in our ***A Celebration of Life Planner: Making Your Memories Your Legacy.***

Education

For each include name of school, city/state, major/degree, graduation date.

High school:

Community college or trade school:

University/College:

Postgraduate degree(s):

Membership in Alumni Association(s):

Career Highlights

Note companies worked for/dates, achievements, awards, etc.

Organizations to Contact

Organizations often play a very important part in our lives, from professional roles to volunteer work. List those you would like notified. This can include unions, fraternal organizations, professional interest groups, volunteer services, and other community contacts.

Note with an asterisk* if you'd like to name any of these organizations as a memorial donation beneficiary.

ORGANIZATION	MY ROLE	CONTACT	YEARS INVOLVED

Newspapers or Publications for Obituary

I would like a death notice or obituary to be published in the following:

Publication:

Publication:

Publication:

Alumni Association(s):

47

Family Tree

One of the most overlooked pieces of information omitted is a simple list of those who came before and after us. Our lineage is unique and to be celebrated. This list can also serve as an easy reference of those to contact and/or include in the obituary.

My parents:

My step-parents:

My grandparents:
- Mother's side:

- Father's side:

My spouse:

My life partner:

My children:

My grandchildren:

My siblings:

My aunts & uncles:

My godparents:

Special Friends to Notify

The following should include those you hold close and those who can be called on to lend support and relay information to others.

NAME	RELATIONSHIP	PHONE	CITY & STATE

TO MY LOVED ONES ~

I have spent much time and put considerable thought into completing this workbook. My intention is one of pure love in the hopes of easing your pain when I am gone. Cherish the memories we made and the time spent together.

_____

Signature

> *When you are sorrowful look again in your heart, and you shall see that in truth you are weeping for that which has been your delight.*
>
> ~Kahlil Gibran

Author Bio

Felicia Barlow Clar is a Sacred Life Celebrant, award-winning producer and writer. She has produced hundreds of corporate and private events, festivals, and award winning videos. For more than 25 years, she has explored deeply spirituality, metaphysics, transformation and self awareness work.

Felicia combined these two facets of her life when, in less than a year and half, she lost both her beloved stepfather and sister. Wanting to celebrate them and their unique contributions, she was able to bring her event expertise to the funeral home process and personalize their memorials, which included dancing at the end of her sister's service. She transformed the experience from suffering to gratitude and joy.

She is the creator of Epilogue Tributes, a niche event company supporting the bereaved with memorial planning and celebrations of life, workbooks, and consulting on end-of-life options. She has received end-of-life CareDoula® education from Quality of Life Care. She has been published in *Elephant Journal,* and her production credits include NBC, HBO, E!, Food Network, Discovery, and PBS.

www.ingramcontent.com/pod-product-compliance
Lightning Source LLC
Chambersburg PA
CBHW080351170426
43194CB00014B/2746